Date: 9/6/22

**3650 Summit Boulevard
West Palm Beach, FL 33406**

10 20L

MAIL TRUCKS

WORKING TRUCKS

PAUL ZACHARY

www.usps.com

EZ READERS

Creating Young Nonfiction Readers

EZ Readers lets children delve into nonfiction at beginning reading levels. Young readers are introduced to new concepts, facts, ideas, and vocabulary.

Tips for Reading Nonfiction with Beginning Readers

Talk about Nonfiction
Begin by explaining that nonfiction books give us information that is true. The book will be organized around a specific topic or idea, and we may learn new facts through reading.

Look at the Parts
Most nonfiction books have helpful features. Our *EZ Readers* include a Contents page, an index, a picture glossary, and color photographs. Share the purpose of these features with your reader.

Contents
Located at the front of a book, the Contents displays a list of the big ideas within the book and where to find them.

Index
An index is an alphabetical list of topics and the page numbers where they are found.

Picture Glossary
Located at the back of the book, a picture glossary contains key words/phrases that are related to the topic.

Photos/Charts
A lot of information can be found by "reading" the charts and photos found within nonfiction text. Help your reader learn more about the different ways information can be displayed.

With a little help and guidance about reading nonfiction, you can feel good about introducing a young reader to the world of *EZ Readers* nonfiction books.

Mitchell Lane
PUBLISHERS

2001 SW 31st Avenue
Hallandale, FL 33009
www.mitchelllane.com

First Edition, 2019.

Author: Paul Zachary
Designer: Ed Morgan
Editor: Sharon F. Doorasamy

Names/credits:
Title: Mail Trucks / by Paul Zachary
Description: Hallandale, FL : Mitchell Lane Publishers, [2019]

Series: Working Trucks

Library bound ISBN: 9781680203004

eBook ISBN: 9781680203011

EZ readers is an imprint of Mitchell Lane Publishers

Photo credits: Getty Images, Freepik.com

CONTENTS

A mail truck is a **delivery vehicle** that is used to deliver the mail.

The mail truck used by the United States Postal Service is the same truck that has been used since the late 1980s.

Mail trucks are custom-made. They are 175 inches (440 cm) long, weigh 3,000 pounds (1,400 kg) and can carry up to 1,000 pounds (450 kg) of mail.

Mail carriers that work in urban areas walk door-to-door to hand deliver mail.

The mail truck has a right-handed driver's position with a tray that holds mail on the other side.

The mail carrier can easily grab sorted mail and place it into **mailboxes** without having to leave the seat.

911

The back of the mail truck has plenty of room for trays of mail.

Mail trucks deliver mail to homes and businesses. They also take **outgoing** mail to the **post office** to be delivered around the country.

19

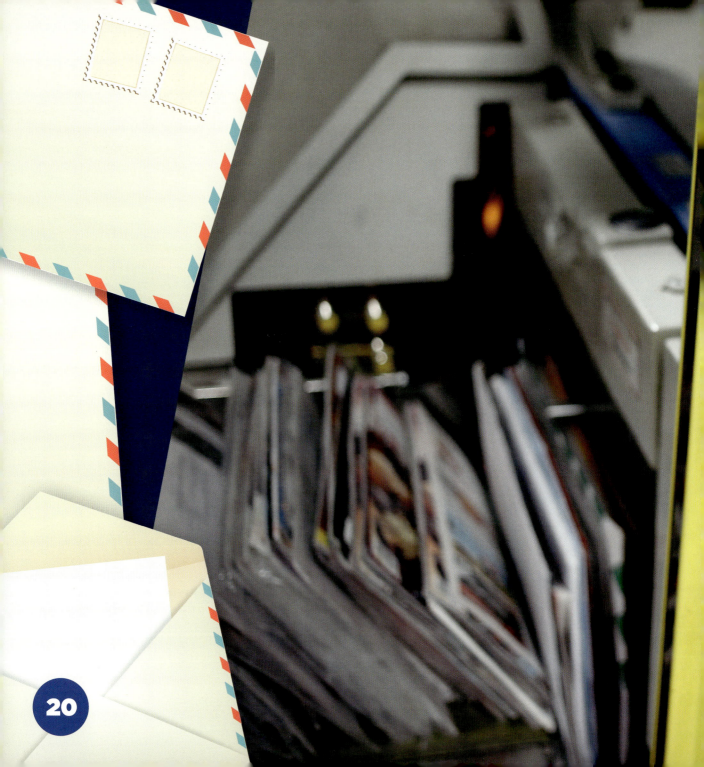

Workers at the post office place **letters** in big **sorting machines** to help send letters where they must go.

21

GLOSSARY

delivery
To bring to the proper place

letters
A written message addressed to a person or company

mailboxes
A public box in which mail is placed for pickup and delivery

outgoing
Letters that are addressed and ready to be mailed

post office
A building where you can buy stamps and pick-up or drop-off mail

sorting machines
Large machines that separates letters for different locations

vehicle
A machine that is used to carry goods from one place to another

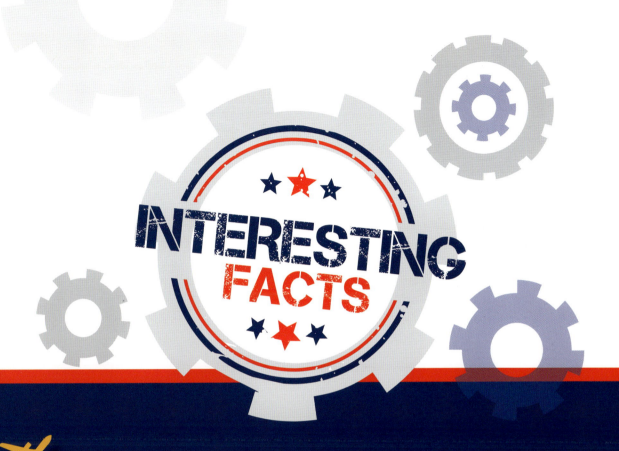

INTERESTING FACTS

The earliest mail carriers went on foot, by horse, or in carriages. Later, mail traveled by train or steamboats. Today, it goes mostly by planes and trucks.

Today you can send a message to someone by text or e-mail in an instant. Two hundred years ago people waited for weeks for a letter from family or friends.

INDEX